SCIENCE ! SLEUTHS

?

PROVE IT!

SHIRLEY DUKE

Crabtree Publishing Company

www.crabtreebooks.com

SCIENCE SLEUTHS

Author
Shirley Duke

Publishing plan research and development
Reagan Miller

Editor
Kathy Middleton

Proofreader and indexer
Crystal Sikkens

Photo research
Samara Parent

Design
Samara Parent

Print and production coordinator
Margaret Amy Salter

Prepress technician:
Tammy McGarr

Photographs
Shutterstock: © Scott Prokop p 17
Thinkstock: TOC, p 5, 6, 7 (top right), 8, 10, 20 ,21 (center)

All other images by Shutterstock

Library and Archives Canada Cataloguing in Publication

Duke, Shirley Smith, author
   Prove it! / Shirley Duke.

(Science sleuths)
Includes index.
Issued in print and electronic formats.
ISBN 978-0-7787-1543-6 (bound).--ISBN 978-0-7787-1547-4 (pbk.).--
ISBN 978-1-4271-1595-9 (pdf).--ISBN 978-1-4271-1591-1 (html)

   1. Science--Methodology--Juvenile literature. 2. Experimental
design--Juvenile literature. I. Title.

Q175.2.D854 2015   j507.2   C2015-901528-6
                                          C2015-901529-4

Library of Congress Cataloging-in-Publication Data

Duke, Shirley Smith, author.
 Prove it! / Shirley Duke.
   pages cm. -- (Science sleuths)
 Includes index.
 ISBN 978-0-7787-1543-6 (reinforced library binding : alk. paper) --
ISBN 978-0-7787-1547-4 (pbk. : alk. paper) --
ISBN 978-1-4271-1595-9 (electronic pdf : alk. paper) --
ISBN 978-1-4271-1591-1 (electronic html : alk. paper)
1. Science--Methodology--Juvenile literature. 2. Science--Experiments--Juvenile
literature. 3. Scientists--Juvenile literature. I. Title.

 Q175.2.D86 2015
 507.2--dc23
                 2015008989

Crabtree Publishing Company

Printed in the U.S.A./062015/CJ20150512

www.crabtreebooks.com   1-800-387-7650

Published in Canada
Crabtree Publishing
616 Welland Ave.
St. Catharines, Ontario
L2M 5V6

Published in the United States
Crabtree Publishing
PMB 59051
350 Fifth Avenue, 59th Floor
New York, New York 10118

Published in the United Kingdom
Crabtree Publishing
Maritime House
Basin Road North, Hove
BN41 1WR

Published in Australia
Crabtree Publishing
3 Charles Street
Coburg North
VIC 3058

CONTENTS

HOW DO YOU KNOW FOR SURE?

You and your friend wonder how to split a jar containing green and pink candies evenly. Your friend looks at the jar and says he'll take the green ones because it looks like there are probably the same number of each color. But you want to know for sure. You suggest sorting them by color and counting them. You are thinking just like a scientist!

Scientists are people who study the **natural world**. The natural world is made of all the living and nonliving things around us. Scientists are **curious**. This means they are interested in learning about new things. Scientists want to **explain**, or give reasons, why things happen the way they do in the natural world. But how do they know what the best explanation is? They use **facts** to prove it.

Some scientists study plants and learn about how they grow.

INVESTIGATIONS

Scientists learn about the world by asking questions. They might ask these sorts of questions:

What does a seed need to grow?

How does a snake move?

Scientists do **investigations** to answer their questions. An investigation is a way of gathering information. Investigations can be done by making **observations**. An observation is information gathered using your senses, such as sight, hearing, taste, touch, and smell.

Investigations can also be done by sorting things into groups or doing an **experiment**, or test. The kind of investigation a scientist does depends on the kind of questions he or she wants to answer. Investigations allow scientists to gather as much information on a subject as they can.

A SCIENTIST ASKS:

Which bounces higher—a golf ball or a tennis ball? To answer this question, the scientist does an experiment. Both balls are dropped from the same height. The scientist watches and measures how high each ball bounces to find the answer.

WHAT IS DATA?

The information scientists collect during investigations is called **data**. Data includes every fact that has been observed. This information is recorded by the scientist and used to help answer his or her question. Just like scientists, we use our five senses to gather information.

Things to observe

- what different beak shapes look like

- which kinds of birds have different beak shapes

- what kind of foods they eat

Look up average size of each bird in reference book

What I saw at the bird sanctuary

- hummingbird:
a long beak like a tube
— ate nectar from flowers

- woodpecker:
a strong beak that pecked at wood like a chisel
— ate insects in treebark

- hawk:
a short, hooked beak
— ate live prey

- grosbeak
a cone-shaped beak
— ate seeds

QUESTION:

Why do birds have different beak shapes?

?

WHAT IS EVIDENCE?

Evidence is the set of facts from the data gathered that supports a scientist's answer. Not all the data collected is evidence. Only the data used by the scientist to answer the question is evidence.

The answer, or **conclusion**, is something that can be observed, demonstrated, or supported with evidence.

CONCLUSION:
The shape of a bird's beak helps it eat a certain kind of food more easily.

Scientists put data in a form they can use, such as charts or graphs. Then they look for patterns, or causes and effects. The data here shows evidence of a connection between beak shape and food.

Data Collected on Bird Beaks

Picture	Beak Description	Kind of Bird	Food	Length of Bird
	beak is long, like a tube	hummingbird	drinks nectar deep inside flowers	3–4" (7.5–10 cm)
	strong beak like a chisel	woodpecker	pecks out insects under tree bark	16–19" (40–48 cm)
	sharp beak with hook	hawk	captures live prey in beak	18–26" (46–66 cm)
	strong, cone-shaped beak	grosbeak	cracks seeds with beak	6–9" (15–23 cm)

9

IS IT A FACT OR AN OPINION?

Scientists use facts as evidence. A fact is something that can be proven to be true. For example, if you drop something, it will fall toward the ground or floor. This is a fact. Objects fall downward because a force called gravity pulls them in that direction. Even if you don't know about gravity, you can demonstrate that this is true by dropping different items yourself. You have proven that this fact is true.

Even feathers will float downward when dropped.

An **opinion** is a personal feeling or belief about something. Opinions are statements that cannot be proven by facts. You can say that a sunny day is nicer than a rainy day. Is this true for everyone or just you? Other people may like rainy days better, so it is not a fact.

EXPLORE IT!

?

Read each sentence below. Is it a fact or an opinion? Please explain your thinking.

1. Bees can sting.
2. Sharks are scary.
3. Summer is the best season.
4. Water turns into ice when it gets very cold.

Birds make better pets than dogs. This is an opinion because it cannot be proven. Some people may think dogs make better pets than birds. An opinion cannot be proven with evidence.

WHAT IS AN ARGUMENT?

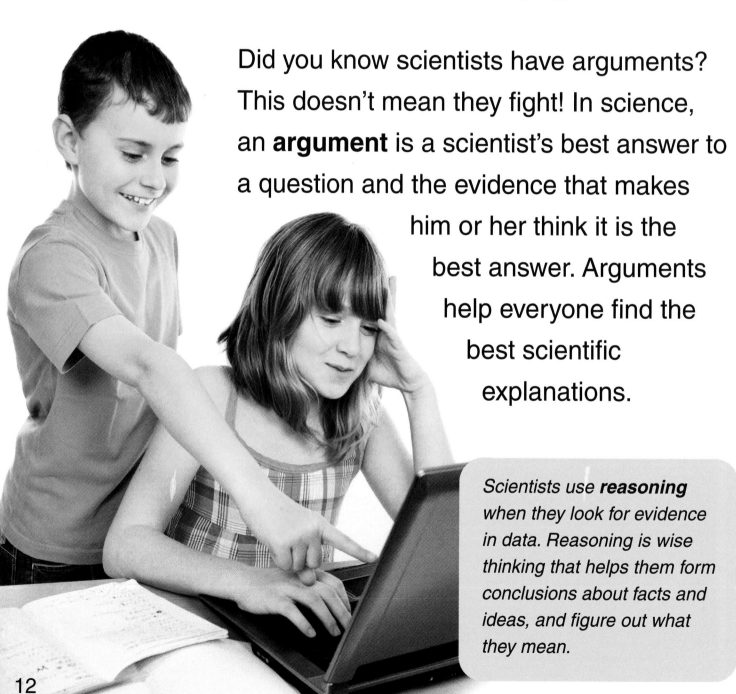

Did you know scientists have arguments? This doesn't mean they fight! In science, an **argument** is a scientist's best answer to a question and the evidence that makes him or her think it is the best answer. Arguments help everyone find the best scientific explanations.

*Scientists use **reasoning** when they look for evidence in data. Reasoning is wise thinking that helps them form conclusions about facts and ideas, and figure out what they mean.*

An argument is made up of two parts—a conclusion and evidence. A conclusion is a scientist's best answer and must be something that can be observed, demonstrated, or supported with evidence. A conclusion supported with evidence makes it hard to argue that a different conclusion is more correct.

A scientist might form the conclusion that bird beaks are different because they eat different kinds of food.

A scientist that observes birds eating, will see birds that drink nectar have long, thin beaks to reach inside flowers. He or she will also see birds that eat seeds have strong, thick beaks to crack them open.

SUPPORTING THE ARGUMENT

These young scientists want to do an investigation to learn more about how light helps plants grow. They start by asking a question: Is a plant's height and number of leaves affected by how much light it receives? They plan and carry out an investigation.

They put one plant under a light for 24 hours every day for a week. They put the same size and kind of plant under a light for 12 hours every day for a week. They collect their data to help them answer this question.

Height	Mon.	Tues.	Wed.	Thurs.	Fri.	Sat.	Sun.
24 hrs	1 in. (2.54 cm)	2 in. (5 cm)	3 in. (7.6 cm)	4 in. (10.1 cm)	5 in. (12.7 cm)	5 1/2 in. (13.9 cm)	6 in. (15.2 cm)
12 hrs	1 in. (2.54 cm)	1 1/2 in. (3.8 cm)	2 in. (5 cm)	2 1/4 in. (5.7 cm)	2 1/2 in. (6.3 cm)	2 3/4 in. (6.9 cm)	3 in. (7.6 cm)

Leaves	Mon.	Tues.	Wed.	Thurs.	Fri.	Sat.	Sun.
24 hrs	2	3	5	7	9	10	12
12 hrs	2	2	3	4	5	6	7

The data shows the plant that received 24 hours of light every day grew six inches (15.2 cm) tall and has 12 leaves. The plant that received 12 hours of light grew only three inches (7.6 cm) and has only seven leaves.

The young scientists draw the conclusion that the height and number of leaves of a plant is affected by the amount of light it gets. The height and number of leaves increases as the amount of light increases. The evidence from the data supports their conclusion. The plant that received more light grew taller and has more leaves.

EXPLORE IT!

?

Can you draw a conclusion from the data below? What is your evidence that your conclusion is correct?

A boy wonders if an object is hollow, will it float? He sees that a beach ball floats in his pool, but a water balloon sinks.

SCIENTISTS SHARE INFORMATION

Scientists share their conclusions with other scientists. They also share their evidence. Sharing information allows other scientists to use it in their own investigations. They can repeat the same investigation or investigate different parts of that idea. More information is learned by sharing.

Sharing results lets other scientists repeat your investigation. When your work is repeated and the results are the same, it shows your work is based on evidence. No one knew about gravity until Sir Isaac Newton wrote about it. Other scientists carried out his tests and the results were always the same.

The idea that all living things are made of cells, the smallest unit of life, was discovered over 150 years ago. Later, other scientists learned that cells have tiny parts that make them work.

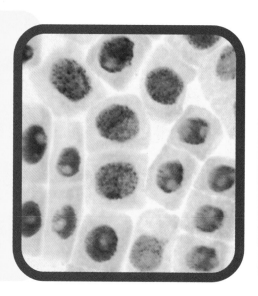

Scientists share their conclusions in different ways. They may write reports in science magazines. Experts read their reports and use the information.

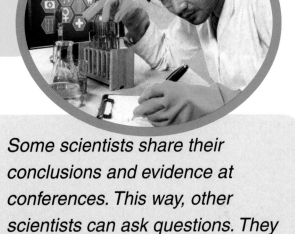

Some scientists share their conclusions and evidence at conferences. This way, other scientists can ask questions. They work as a community to learn more. They argue to find the best evidence for conclusions.

Others present the information at universities. They discuss their information. Sharing ideas leads to better evidence and sometimes even new ideas.

RESPECT THROUGH QUESTIONS

Scientists do not always agree with one another, but they always show respect to other scientists. They listen carefully, then work to investigate the information. Not only is listening good manners, it might also give them a new idea to investigate. They may disagree, but they listen well.

Scientists expect questions from other scientists. Being able to explain his or her thinking makes sure a scientist's work is as correct as possible.

Good, respectful questions help everyone understand the ideas better. Asking "How do you know?" makes scientists review their work and show it was correct information. Good questions ask things like these:

- *How does your evidence support your conclusion?*
- *How many times did you repeat your investigation?*
- *Did anything happen that you could not explain?*
- *What is the importance of your conclusion?*
- *May I see your data?*

Scientists present their evidence when talking to other scientists or writing about it. They speak about it like this:

Scientists may have different ideas about the evidence that has been presented. They argue, but word it with respect.

The evidence I use to support _____ is _____.
I believe _____ (statement) because _____ (reasoning).
I know that _____ is _____ because _____
Based on _____, I think _____.

I disagree _____ because _____. The reason I believe _____ is _____.
The facts that support my idea are _____.

MATCHING EVIDENCE

People, animals, and plants change their **environments** to meet their needs. They do this for many reasons. People and animals change their environments to make shelter, grow or find food, and keep safe. Plants grow in soil that has the **nutrients** they need. Their roots spread out to reach the nutrients.

Use the pictures on both pages as evidence to support each of the three conclusions listed below. Match the pictures to the conclusions:

1. Animals change the environment.

2. Plants change the environment.

3. People change the environment.

Make observations from your own environment and add them as evidence to one of the three conclusions. Make observations in your back yard, local park, your school yard, or around your neighborhood.

PROVE IT YOURSELF!

The goal of a scientist is to prove his or her answer is the best one possible. She does this by basing her conclusion on evidence. Scientists must always be able to explain their conclusions.

Scientists investigate an idea in different ways. They gather facts, which are their data. The group of facts from the data that supports their idea becomes the scientists' evidence.

Evidence is used to draw a conclusion. Scientists make an argument using their conclusion and evidence to show that their idea is correct.

Scientists do not use opinions. Opinions are based on feelings, not evidence. Scientists use reasoning at every step in their work to give the best possible answer to the question they are investigating.

LEARNING MORE

BOOKS

What Do We Know Now? Drawing Conclusions and Answering the Question by Robin Johnson. Crabtree Publishing Company, 2010.

Up, Up in a Balloon. by Lawrence F. Lowery. NSTA Kids, 2013.

The Everything Kids' Science Experiments Book by Tom Robinson. Adams Media, 2001.

WEBSITES

Find an idea to test and work like a scientist.
https://explorable.com/kids-science-projects

This site explains how to begin making a scientific argument.
http://undsci.berkeley.edu/article/coreofscience_01

Visit this site to learn about plants, animals, weather, energy, and much more!
http://easyscienceforkids.com/

GLOSSARY

Note: Some boldfaced words are defined where they appear in the text.

argument (AHR-gyuh-muh nt) noun An evidence-based way to describe what a scientist thinks and why

conclusion (kuh n-KLOO-zhuh n) noun A statement based on evidence from data

curious (KYOO-R-ee-uh-s) adjective Interested in learning about new things

data (DEY-tuh) noun Facts gathered from an investigation

environment (en-VAHY-ruh n-muh nt) noun Surroundings of a living thing

evidence (EV-i-duh-ns) noun A collected set of facts that support a scientist's conclusion

explain (ik-SPLEYN) verb To give a reason why something happens the way it does

fact (FAKT) noun A statement that can be shown as true

natural world (NACH-er-uhl WURLD) noun All the living and nonliving things around us

nutrient (NOO-tree-uh nt) noun A natural substance that living things need for growth and good health

opinion (uh-PIN-yuh n) noun What someone thinks or feels about something

reasoning (REE-zuh-ning) verb Wise thinking to form conclusions about facts, ideas, and what they mean

An adjective is a word that describes what something is like.
A noun is a person, place, or thing.
A verb is an action word that tells you what someone or something does.

INDEX